Tools to Prevent Burnout

The Invigorate Model

I0096300

Katarina Gaborova

Tools to Prevent Burnout: The Invigorate Model
Katarina Gaborova © 2024

4.37" x 7" (178 mm x 111 mm)

Petra Books
petrabooks.ca

Front cover drawing and interior drawings by Zuzana Mažonasová. A versatile professional with a background in both web and graphic design currently designing and managing merchandise for the popular Slovakian podcast *Vražedné Psyché,* Mažonasová collaborated with Katarína Gaborova on V!VA Tools for Well-being (Slovak version), as well as managing the SeeBeeTee (Cognitive Behavioral Therapy) products. More at www.mdgroup.sk.

Greetings

To anyone who has felt the heavy weight of burnout, whether it has impacted your professional life, your relationships, or your personal well-being, this book is dedicated to you and your loved ones.

The following statistics may surprise you, but they are shared not to alarm, but to highlight the urgent need for change in our work environments. It's time to slow down and prioritize the overall well-being of all employees. Happy and healthy employees are efficient, productive, and can drive your workplaces to heights you haven't even imagined.

In January 2020, before the pandemic, burnout statistics among U.S. employees were already alarming, with rates ranging from 24% to 53%. A year later, in February 2021, these numbers had risen significantly across all generations: 58% of Generation Z, 59% of Millennials, 54% of Generation X, and 31% of Baby Boomers experiencing burnout (Statista Research Department, 2021), clearly show the increasing prevalence of burnout.

I hope this book acknowledges your experiences, validates your challenges, while offering support and practical suggestions to help you achieve a much better work-life balance and overall well-being.

K.G.

Testimonials

Louiza:

"Burnout challenged me, a 26 year old female, in a way I had never experienced before. My financial stress, 6-day work schedule, and no sense of fulfillment in professional/personal matters were major factors causing my burnout. Working harder over a long period of time resulted in a psychological meltdown. My energy levels so decreased that simple tasks became very hard. I did not feel like myself anymore, and my physical and mental health became very poor. I sought professional advice. Katarina and I met on a weekly basis, and throughout our sessions I learned a lot about how burnout works and what to do to combat it.

Therapy helped me to articulate the issue and discuss new perspectives and methods of handling the complexity of the issue. I practiced meditation and breathing exercises. I forced myself to take breaks throughout the day; I turned to journaling and wrote down my thoughts when I felt overwhelmed; I had a lot of "I should" thoughts, I started challenging them, and things got a bit easier. Letting go of my ego and high self-expectations was tough but necessary. I also started paying more attention to what I was eating and taking vitamin supplements, which boosted my energy levels. I had some weeks off which allowed me the time to step back and recharge. At home, I offloaded some household chores to my partner, and signed up to a grocery home delivery service. Lastly, talking openly with friends and family about what I was going through also provided a lot of support. These combined changes helped me start feeling like myself again."

Carolyn:

"After recovering from burnout, I realised how long I had been sailing close to the wind. I never thought I would be 'one of those people'. It wasn't one event that had got me to that point but years of doing just a little more. Therapy made me appreciate that I cannot control everything, something that took me time to accept. The 'bilateral stimulation' of EMDR (Eye Movement Desensitization and Reprocessing) really helped when I had so many thoughts running through my head. My long term take away and strategy has been appreciating the power of saying no and creating clear boundaries between work and home. Over time even my colleagues know that when I leave the building I leave work too. No emails or communication! It took years to reach burnout. Returning to the status quo is not the goal."

Craig:

"I didn't believe in burnout until about 3 months ago. A senior manager in my late 20s, I quickly rose through the ranks of teaching after retraining in my 30s. I have lived in several different countries with each of my careers and have a wife and two children. I know stress, have felt it and dealt with it. My new job in a new country seemed like another fun challenge; it was to prove one challenge too far.

My first symptom was a horrible pain in my jaw, although I didn't know when it first occurred. The second symptom I noticed was catastrophizing, ruminating in endless loops, none of which ended well. I had lots of time to think about it, usually at 2:40 am every night and again at 5:40 am. The third symptom was sleeplessness or disturbed sleep. It had been happening for so long, that it became the norm. Feeling something was wrong, I made an appointment with my doctor. Before my visit, all of this caught up with me, resulting in an enormous panic attack... while at work with chest pain and tightening, uncontrollable thoughts, and frightening blood pressure readings...

(Craig continued): I had had a lucky escape physically, but mentally, I was ill. I struggled to accept this and tried to carry on. I agreed to half days, gave up some responsibility and cracked on as tough professional people do. It took a very strong, caring and understanding line manager to take me aside and insist, for my own health, that I take some time to heal as it was clear I couldn't perform at my best.

The best things my organization have done to support me are to:

➤ Listen to me and understand burnout,
➤ Provide ongoing medical MH support through a supportive HR department,
➤ Put support in place quickly and insist I take time to heal,
➤ Allowed and encouraged me to step back completely, even when I didn't want to."

Maylon Rojer, project manager:

"Ever take a course, which seemed super relevant yet you do not really have the chance to put in practice what you have learned? Over time that knowledge fades. In my opinion education for employees is very important, however, it should be equally important for those employees to use that knowledge or get updates over the course of time. From my observation at work, I have seen one lecture/presentation on burnout during the past three years. Over those same 3 years I have witnessed at least three burnouts.

Active burnout prevention would be beneficial to my organization, and its employees, and looking at the statistics the same applies to many other organizations. Interactive sessions, with hands-on practice and personal stories of what led to burnout, would make the experience more engaging and memorable. Having a creative workshop with updated information once a year would continue to make it more relevant, really drive down its occurrence, and instill a cultural change and awareness within organizations."

Gaborova

Table of Contents

Gaborova

Tools to Prevent Burnout:
The Invigorate Model

Burnout, what is it really?

Have you been feeling emotionally and physically exhausted? Do you find yourself trapped in a cycle of endless chores, irritability, sleeplessness, and dark thoughts? You may have lost motivation, found yourself blaming yourself and others more than usual, and struggled with feelings of inadequacy. Are you increasingly aware of various stressors that seem to be piling up, leaving you feeling overwhelmed? No matter how much effort, overtime, energy, or resources you put into your work, does it seem like there is no end in sight, or worse, that you are not good enough? If this has been going on for a prolonged period, you might be wondering, "How did I get on this high-speed train, and will there ever be a stop so I can finally get off?" You know what I'm talking about, especially during those moments when you try to slow down and catch your breath, only to realize that your body can no longer relax.

These could be symptoms of burnout. According to the 11th Revision of the International Classification of Diseases (ICD-11), burnout is classified as an occupational phenomenon, and is not considered a medical condition.

The World Health Organization (WHO, 2019) characterized burn-out syndrome as "a result from chronic workplace stress that has not been successfully managed".

Is burnout solely work-related?

Although burnout is commonly associated with work-related stress, it's not exclusively tied to the workplace. It can occur in various aspects of life, such as caregiving responsibilities, academic pursuits, even personal relationships, highlighting that any prolonged period of stress, pressure, or exhaustion can eventually lead to burn-out. For this reason, it is crucial to recognize the symptoms of burnout and address them holistically, by reviewing all aspects of life that could have contributed to it.

Dimensions of burnout according to researchers

Burnout is characterized by three dimensions (Maslach & Leiter, 2016):

- Emotional exhaustion: feeling of energy depletion or exhaustion; no matter how much you rest, your body feels drained and emotionally exhausted;
- Depersonalization: increased mental distance from one's job, or feelings of negativism or cynicism related to one's job; and
- Lack of personal accomplishment: reduced professional efficacy.

Deciphering Burnout
as a Physiological Response

Since burnout is not a physical or mental illness, yet affects us both physically and emotionally, how can we make sense of it? Burnout could be visualized as an extreme end of a three stress-related concept on a continuous spectrum, where on one end lies general stress. Defined as a typical physiological and emotional reaction to everyday demands or changes in the environment.

Stages of Stress - Acute stress (Stage 1)

Stress occurs in three stages. The first stage, known as acute stress, is the initial response to a stressor characterized by the rapid release of adrenaline, which triggers the fight-or-flight response with increased heart rate and heightened alertness. This response is crucial for organisms to cope with immediate threats or challenges. Shortly after, cortisol, a steroid hormone, is released to sustain the body's response over a more extended period by increasing blood sugar levels, suppressing non-essential bodily functions, and enhancing cardiovascular function (Zafar et al., 2021). Cortisol affects nearly every organ in the body, eventually returning to baseline once the stress subsides (Sparks, 2021). An example of acute stress is the arousal experienced when crossing a busy street to avoid oncoming cars.

Chronic stress (Stage 2)

Chronic stress arises when stress persists for prolonged periods at high intensity. This stage involves a prolonged conflict process where the body continuously tries to manage the stressor. Chronic stress leads to sustained cortisol release, which can overwhelm the body emotionally and physically, affecting health and hindering the return to a resting state. Cortisol secretion becomes dysregulated, sometimes taking weeks to normalize (Karin et al., 2020). An example of chronic stress is enduring a demanding work environment with unmanageable pressure.

Burnout and its' sliding scale (Stage 3)

Burnout can be viewed as the final stage of chronic stress. This exhaustion phase, occurs when the body has exhausted all its resources. It manifests as emotional exhaustion, where individuals feel drained and unable to cope emotionally and physically. Depersonalization follows, characterized by a detached response towards work, having a negative outlook and a cynical attitude. Lastly, reduced personal accomplishment sets in, where individuals feel that no matter how hard they work, there is a lack of achievement and productivity.

During this phase the body eventually depletes its own resources and can no longer function effectively. The physiological impact is that cortisol levels in severely affected individuals may exhibit hypocortisolism. Also known as adrenal insufficiency "hypocorticism", it is characterized by insufficient production of cortisol by the adrenal glands (Lennartsson, 2015). Since cortisol is a vital hormone regulating various bodily functions, including metabolism, immune response, and stress response, it starts affecting one's overall health and well-being (Thau et.al., 2023).

What are the common symptoms of burnout?

- Chronic fatigue (persists despite physical rest)
- Decreased immunity (colds, illness, inflammation)
- Insomnia (disrupted sleep patterns)
- Physical symptoms (body aches, tension)
- Emotional exhaustion
- Reduced performance (due to feeling overwhelmed/exhaustion)
- Withdrawal from responsibilities (blocked decision-making processes, focus, motivation)
- Loss of enjoyment (loss of laughter, humor and pleasurable activities)
- Increased cynicism (having a negative filter in the mind)
- Feeling overwhelmed (what task to start first, how to start it and choosing priorities), and
- Poor self-care

These symptoms can be experienced and may overlap during all stages of stress and burnout. However, there are usually different experiences of these symptoms in their increased level of intensity, the reaction to the stressors as well as a response to applied treatment. This is especially evident the closer one is to the burnout end of the continuous stress scale. For example, exercise is a great general remedy for stress, however during the burnout stage one needs to be more gentle with the type, duration and intensity of the exercise. Similar differences apply to diet, amount of rest, and social activities. For this reason, it is strongly recommended to get individually fitted guidance from a health care professional (such as a psychologist, physiotherapist, nutritionist, and medical doctor).

Burnout Effect on the Brain

Research findings indicate that burnout can lead to alterations in the neural circuits of the brain. Specifically, individuals experiencing burnout often exhibit an enlarged amygdala, a brain region associated with emotional responses, as observed in R-fMRI studies. These individuals also demonstrate weakened connections between the amygdala and the anterior cingulate cortex, linked to emotional distress, as well as diminished correlations between amygdala activity and the medial prefrontal cortex, responsible for executive functioning.

Due to these neural changes, burnout may result in difficulties regulating negative emotions, thereby negatively affecting cognitive abilities such as attention, memory retention, and learning, which in turn increase the likelihood of errors and fostering negative perceptions of work-related stress (Golkar et al., 2014; Arnsten & Shanafelt,2021). Another intriguing finding from brain research is that uncontrollable stress, "involving situations where the individual has little to no control over the stressor", is leading to significant negative changes in brain circuits. While the controllable stress "involves stressors that an individual can manage or influence", typically does not cause significant changes in brain circuits (Arnsten & Shanafelt, 2021).

According to Arnsten and Shanafelt (2021), uncontrollable stress causes the synaptic connections in the prefrontal cortex to deteriorate, while connections in more primitive brain areas expand, supporting also Golkar's et.al, (2014) fMRI finding. This also explains how uniquely, uncontrollable stress affects our brains, after triggering release of high levels of chemicals (norepinephrine, dopamine, and acetylcholine), thus weakening the function of the prefrontal cortex, regulating thoughts, actions, and emotions. This further diminishes a variety of abilities that people who experience burnout often complain about including feeling negative impact on their abstract thinking, decision-making, and perseverance.

Fortunately, both the aforementioned experiences and neurological changes can be reversed with appropriate care, such as sustained and regular self-care practices, lifestyle improvements, bolstering supportive social networks, and minimizing stressors where possible. Having an appropriate assessment by a medical doctor and a mental health professional are recommended as the first stepping stones towards recovery.

Methodology

As a psychologist, I meet many clients who describe having feelings and thoughts of "not being a good enough person", "not being able to accomplish things" and accusing themselves of turning into "lazy and unmotivated versions of themselves", not realizing that those thoughts of worthlessness, helplessness and downward-spiral feelings were caused by prolonged stress. While searching for the right support for my clients, I researched a number of theories upon which the Invigorate Model is based:

- The Job Demand-Control Model proposed by Karasek (1985) and expanded upon by Van der Doef and Maes (1999), suggests that job strain arises from the interaction between high job demands and low levels of job control. Highlighting that if individuals face high demands but little autonomy in their work, they are more prone to stress and adverse health outcomes. The model postulates that balancing workload and decision-making authority is important in reducing workplace stress.
- The Conservation of Resources Theory, developed by Hobfoll (1989) and later expanded by Halbesleben and Buckley (2004), proposes that individuals strive to acquire and maintain resources (e.g energy, time, and social support). Stress occurs when individuals perceive a threat of resource loss or experience actual resource loss, resulting in efforts to protect or replenish these resources in order to maintain well-being.
- The Job-Demands-Resources Model, developed by Demerouti, et.al. (2001), proposes that job characteristics may include two categories: job demands and job resources. According to this theory,

high job demands along with low job resources lead to burnout and other negative outcomes. On the other hand, high job resources can buffer the impact of job demands and reinforce work engagement and well-being.

- The Transactional Model, proposed by Lazarus and Folkman (1984), postulates that stress arises from the interaction between individuals and their environment. Specifically, stress is perceived as a result of the two types of appraisal processes. These cognitive appraisals suggest that how individuals perceive and interpret stressors in turn influences their emotional and behavioral responses, and also, shape their adaptation to stressful situations.

- The Work-life Model, by Leiter and Maslach (1999), emphasizes six key domains including:

  1. workload (the volume and intensity of tasks and responsibilities),
  2. control (the degree to which individuals can influence or make decisions about work),
  3. reward (recognition, compensation, and other positive reinforcements for one's efforts),
  4. community (refers to the quality of relationships and social support),
  5. fairness (such as perceptions of equity, justice, and fairness at work), and
  6. values (includes alignment between personal values and work values).

These critical elements help in understanding the experiences of individuals in their work and personal lives, highlighting how balance and satisfaction in both personal and work areas are important. The combination of conflict arising between work and personal life, and deficiencies in one of the domains affecting the other, leads to reduced well-being.

As part of the research, 40 professionals whose work included supporting people suffering from burnout were interviewed; the interviewees had medical or human resources (HR) background: 10 general practitioners, 10 psychologists, 10 physiotherapists and 10 HR professionals.

I discovered that the occurrence of burnout is not only within an organization, an individual, or a work team; rather it is due to a complex interaction of all of them together. Indeed, the remedy needs to include a more holistic approach targeting a support of an individual, team as well as the whole organization. In an individual's life, I focus on minimizing stressors and establishing building blocks which create more energy, strengthen resilience, and invigorate and support all three dimensions simultaneously: the individual, the work team and the employer/ organization.

The Invigorate Model includes support for individuals, teams, and organizations.

Throughout my career I have seen that once individuals reenter their work environment after being off work (for months), if there are no adjustments made at one's work (e.g. less workload, more resources, more flexible deadlines etc.), then the person slides back to burnout typically within months after resuming work. Research also suggests that an individual intervention appears to be partially effective and for a shorter period of time (up to 6 months) (Awa, et.al., 2010; Westermann, et.al., 2014), when compared with organizational support (changes made at work) (McFarland, Hlubocky, & Riba, 2019). Ultimately, if individual burnout is due to a work-related issue, then some changes at work are essential as without them the individual is more likely to relapse.

This 3-dimensional approach (support of an individual/team/workplace) is exactly what the 'INVIGORATE MODEL' guidelines are all about. The Invigorate Model explores over 40 thematic guides, in 3 sections related to the contributing factors and remedies of burnout:

- Section 1: 10 green guides focus on what an employer can do for its employees.
- Section 2: 15 blue guides relate to the support of team leaders / team members.
- Section 3: 18 red guides relate to individual self-care and burnout prevention.

The Invigorate Model is based on the evaluation of the five mentioned theoretical models, combined with the expertise of 40 burnout-reduction professionals. This book shows new ways of coping, provides some understanding and support, and most importantly enhances positive changes to the state of being. While the model is dedicated for prevention of chronic stress and burnout symptoms, it is noteworthy that the guidelines can also be followed as a treatment. However, individuals requiring help need to seek the guidance of a health care professional (e.g. physician, psychologist, physiotherapists, etc.) to determine the duration and intensity, conduct an assessment of the stressors, manage their reduction, and build individual buffers to induce an intervention. This process requires gentleness and patience as recovery from burnout may take between 6 months to 2 years, depending on how far along an individual is situated on the continuous scale of the final burnout stage.

How to use this book

After reading the book and reviewing the guidelines:

- ➢ Focus on the guidelines that are most relevant to your specific situation;
- ➢ Note that each guideline offers solutions to particular challenges;
- ➢ Develop a personalized plan with specific remedies targeting your issues, keeping in mind that everyone has unique stressors and coping mechanisms. Focus on creating a personalized support plan designed for your individual needs; and finally,
- ➢ Implement the suggestions from the guidelines, following them consistently and regularly for at least 30 days. Adhering to the recommendations for a minimum of 30 days can help establish new habits and improve lifestyle patterns, thereby enhancing overall well-being and contributing to the reduction and prevention of burnout. This aligns with the concept of brain neuroplasticity, as outlined by Goodwin (2023). Neuroplasticity refers to the brain's ability to form new neural connections by strengthening or weakening existing pathways and creating new synapses.

As you navigate through this book, my heartfelt wish is for you to find abundant success in your pursuit of balance, enriched with fulfillment as you embrace the invaluable interventions it offers.

With warm greetings from the Netherlands

Katarina Gaborova,
Registered NIP Psychologist
Founder of K.G. Psychological services
www.katarinagaborova.com
psychologistinthehague.com

The Invigorate Model
for personal and professional life

I   **Invest daily for mental and physical well-being**

N   **Notify someone whenever you need help**

V   **Value qualities that reflect your authentic self**

I   **Inform others of boundaries, be firm**

G   **Grow and learn new ideas that feel rewarding**

O   **Organize and manage your workload**

R   **Reduce any stressors**

A   **Activate and nurture positive relationships**

T   **Take regular breaks, balance work and rest**

E   **Exercise 3-4 times a week for 30 minutes**

These themes are explored in depth throughout the 43 Invigorate guidelines (for individual, team and organizational support).

Invest daily for mental and physical well-being

➤ Eat a healthy diet, take vitamins/supplements suggested by dieticians/naturopaths, drink approximately 2 liters of water per day, plan regular sleep time and sleep hygiene, cut alcohol or substances. These practices form the foundation for a healthy lifestyle, and maintaining vitality.

Notify someone whenever you need help

➤ Ask for help if you are overwhelmed, what are your needs? Determine what to change. Asking for help acknowledges that everyone has limits and it's okay to seek support. Determining what changes are necessary helps you to address the root causes of your feeling overwhelmed, take steps toward effective coping strategies/better stress management, and a greater sense of control over challenging situations.

Value qualities that reflect your authentic self

➤ Be honest to yourself and others. Give your opinion truthfully, decide according to your values (as it is important for your immune system), trust your intuition. As unscientific as intuition sounds, it is a valuable tool in decision-making and problem-solving, drawing on subconscious processing and past experiences. Its reliability though depends on the context, individual expertise, and the complexity of the situation. Thus, balance intuition together with critical thinking and evidence-based reasoning to make the best-informed decisions.

Inform others of boundaries, be firm

➢ Minimize (if possible) toxic situations or people that make you feel unhappy, angry, or frustrated. By asserting physical, emotional and mental boundaries, you protect yourself from over-commitment, resentment, and potential harm. Thus establishing healthier dynamics and preserving your mental and emotional health.

Grow and learn new ideas that feel rewarding

➢ Spend time on activities that you feel passionate about, improve a tiny bit each day, challenge yourself. Boredom and not having challenges decreases productivity and motivation, and increases negative emotions and affect mental health.

Organize and manage your workload

➢ At the end of your work day prepare 'to do' lists for next day (high priorities list with no more than 2-3 tasks per day and "a general list of the rest of tasks"), set priorities, seek resources, plan ahead, practice saying 'no', prioritize, divide big tasks into sub tasks. This practice maximizes productivity, efficiency, reduces stress and promotes progress towards your goals.

Reduce any stressors

➤ Identify your stressors, remove or minimize the stressors, search for solutions, ask for resources. If things are out of control, practice acceptance. Such practices empower you to take proactive steps in managing stress. Practicing acceptance helps to: maintain emotional balance; re-focus energy on aspects of your life that can be controlled; promote well-being; and navigate challenging circumstances with greater ease.

Activate and nurture positive relationships

➤ Build a network of positive, encouraging, supportive people. Being surrounded by positive, encouraging, and supportive individuals can enhance mental and emotional well-being. Providing reassurance, perspective, and practical assistance during stressful moments helps to reinforce feelings of belonging, connection, and resilience.

Take regular breaks, balance work and rest

➢ Apply for example a Pomodoro cycle: work 25 minutes and break for 5 minutes, or work 90 minutes with a longer break. The best cycle of productivity is the one that works for you. Learn active practices of relaxation techniques as they not only reduce stress but also improve cognitive function, enhance emotional regulation, improve sleep, and promote neuroplasticity. Neuroplasticity refers to the brain's ability to reorganize and form new neural connections that are crucial for learning, memory, and adaptation to changing environments.

Exercise 3-4 times a week for 30 minutes

➢ Increase serotonin naturally to reduce stress and anxiety, improve mood, and increase resilience. Exercise promotes serotonin synthesis, release, and signals in the brain; elevating serotonin levels are associated with mood-enhancing effects.

Several factors may contribute to risk of burnout. These factors can be grouped into personality traits, work-related conditions, and lifestyle choices:

Personal Characteristics

Researchers have identified several personal characteristics that may make someone more prone to experiencing burnout. These include:

- Emotional instability: Characterized as exhibiting struggles with coping skills and having challenges with controlling emotions or impulses (Alarcon et al., 2009).
- Lower self-efficacy: A lack of belief in one's ability to achieve goals.
- Lower Confidence levels: Associated with diminished belief in own abilities, skills, judgements, experiencing fear of failure.
- Low openness to new ideas: Resistance to change and new experiences (Magnano et al., 2015).

Personality Traits

- Type A Personality: Type A personality traits are characterized by competitiveness, a sense of urgency, high stress levels, and a strong drive for achievement. Such traits have been associated with increased risk of developing burnout. This is because individuals with Type A personality may have a tendency to set high standards for themselves and others, leading to ongoing stress and fatigue (Scott, 2020).
- Low Extraversion: Low levels of extraversion are characterized by a tendency to be more reserved, quiet in nature, gaining energy from or having a preference for solitude. This personality trait has been

also associated with increased risk of developing burnout.

- Low Conscientiousness where conscientiousness is characterized by orderliness, responsibility, and reliability. Even this trait has been found to make one more susceptible to burnout.

- High Neuroticism: characterized by a tendency to experience negative emotions, such as anxiety, fear, moodiness, worry, envy, frustration, jealousy, and loneliness. Individuals with this personality trait perceive and respond to stressors, with heightened physiological reactions, which can exacerbate their stress (Angelini, 2023; Alarcon et al., 2009). For this reason, this personality trait also increases a risk of experiencing burnout.

- Perfectionism: connected to having excessively high standards and a fear of making mistakes. This pursuit of perfection can lead to stress and burnout, as it often feels like the efforts are never good enough (Scott, 2020).

- Need to feel in Control: characterized by the need to control as many aspects in the work and personal environment as possible. Otherwise, there is a tendency to experience high stress levels and potentially burnout especially when faced with situations that can't be managed for a prolonged period of time.

Interestingly, researchers have also identified connections between specific personality traits and their influence on the experience of burnout across its' three dimensions: emotional exhaustion, depersonalization, and a reduced sense of personal accomplishment. (Alarcon et al., 2009). Just like some of the personality traits may be contributing factors to burnout, their antidotes may serve as a valuable protection. For example, emotional stability has been found to act as safeguard specifically against experiencing emotional exhaustion (Alarcon et al. ,2009).

To conclude this section about individual characteristics, it is crucial to recognize that while certain traits may elevate the risk of burnout, this condition results from a very complex interplay of numerous factors. The environment at work, personal life circumstances, inherent characteristics when it comes to stress responses, and many other elements. Thus, burnout shall never be viewed as a personal shortcoming, but rather as a multifaceted issue requiring understanding and compassion.

Work-Related Conditions

Along with individual characteristics, there are a number of work conditions that may be considered as risk factors for burnout:

- High work load and unmanageable time pressure leading to unmanageable workload may contribute even to high performing employees feeling hopeless, and affecting their self-confidence and self-esteem (Wigert & Agrawal, 2018). Excessive work demands and long working hours can lead to physical and mental exhaustion, making burnout more likely.
- Lack of Control over one's work, such as limited decision-making power or autonomy, can contribute to feelings of helplessness and burnout.
- Inadequate rewards such as a lack of recognition or rewards for hard work can lead to feelings of devaluation and burnout.
- Unfair Treatment at work, biases, favoritism, mistreatment by a co-worker or unfair compensation or policies may also contribute to burnout (Wigert & Agrawal, 2018).
- Lack of Role Clarity linked to the accountability, expectations or targets. If these keep constantly changing, such issues in turn, increase employees' exhaustion (Wigert & Agrawal, 2018).
- Overall insufficient work-life balance.
- Lack of social support or Managerial support may involve lack of communication, lack of empathy, guidance or assistance from the manager or colleagues, which may contribute to employees' sense of isolation and decreased job satisfaction (Wigert & Agrawal, 2018).

Personal lifestyle choices can also become a risk factor that negatively affects burnout.

- Poor self-care such as neglecting regular exercise, unhealthy eating, inadequate sleep and relaxation.
- Lack of social support or negative relationships outside work.
- High level of personal stressors due to financial difficulties, relationship problems, or health issues.
- Mismatch in values may cause a disconnect between personal values and the values of the organization. Imagine as a working parent, one of your most important values is work-life balance, which prioritizes spending quality time with your children, family members, friends, and have enough time to pursue personal enjoyable activities. However, the company you work for values long working hours, round-the-clock availability, often interfering with holidays or weekends. Such mismatch in values may make one more prone to burnout.
- Monotony and boredom due to doing repetitive, monotonous tasks without variety or opportunities for growth. Monotony hinders growth, stimulation and mental challenge. Scientific paper by Willis (2014) explored the concept of boredom from a neuroscientific perspective, and how it negatively affects individuals. More specifically, Willis' paper highlighted that sustained boredom can be viewed as highly stressful experience, as it heightens amygdala activity (a region in the limbic system, responsible for fight or flight response) and disrupts communication with the prefrontal cortex. Thus, impairs higher executive functions such as judgment, planning, and emotional control, also leading to involuntary behavioral responses akin to survival reactions seen in animals and behavioral disengagement in stressed students.

All the above suggestions are based on the five theories previously explained.

Mitigating Factors Preventing or Reducing Burnout

Resilience training for individuals and employees:

➤ Build resilience: Learning and adopting stress management techniques to reinforce regular self-regulation such as mindfulness, muscle tension relaxation, breathing and other coping strategies.
➤ Create supportive work environment: Encourage a collaborative work environment with clear communication and recognition.
➤ Manage time effectively: Learn to manage time effectively, including setting boundaries and prioritizing tasks, to help balance work demands and reduce stress.

Burnout prevention or recovery is complex

The following section shows that the Invigorate Model takes into consideration individual support (shown above) and also emphasizes that each individual has diverse risk factors. If exposed to them for a prolonged period of time individual bodies react to them. The role of each individual is to learn to understand their own risk factors, the bodily responses and how to enhance/learn self-regulation. In order to protect their own boundaries, part of this step involves understanding and communicating to others (colleagues, managers, family members or anyone depending on the setting) when personal limits are reached. Boundaries may be emotional, physical and/or mental, as elaborated below.

Emotional Boundaries and Burnout

The characterization of emotional boundaries entail:

- Understanding how one's emotions and those of others are separate, and shall not cause burden on each other excessively.
- However, individuals may offer empathy and support, without absorbing the emotional weight of others.
- Achieving a balance prevents emotional fatigue and emotional burnout.

Individuals lacking strong emotional boundaries may find themselves constantly drained by others' emotional turmoil, eventually leading to chronic stress and exhaustion (Orloff, 2017; Cloud, 2002).

Physical Boundaries and Burnout

Maintaining one's physical boundaries (space) protects from the stress of intrusions into personal space or unwanted touch, thus, fostering feelings of safety and comfort in relationships, and reducing the potential for stress-related tension.

Mental Boundaries and Burnout

While mental boundaries play a pivotal role in preserving mental well-being, by discerning between their own thoughts and beliefs and those of others, individuals can shield themselves from adopting external negativity or undue criticism, preventing self-doubt and negative thought patterns (Orloff, 2017; Cloud, 2002).

Allow yourself patience and understanding, recognizing that comprehending and setting personal boundaries is a gradual process that unfolds over time. Pay attention to signs of tension, distress, or increased physiological activity (e.g. increased heart rate, shortness of breath) as indicators of crossing those boundaries. Once you're adept at recognizing your limits, the next step involves communicating them to those around you.

The Invigorate cards suggest that managers, colleagues, and the work environment shall share responsibility for supporting these boundaries by respecting them and collaborating on solutions. Workshops for organizations can train managers to offer constructive, solution-based responses, incorporating elements like compassion, empathy, communication, and Cognitive Behavioral Therapy-based techniques.

Symptoms employers need to pay attention to and how they lead to reduced effectiveness.

Initial signs of distress among employees may include diminished effectiveness, reduced work performance, and overall productivity (Korunka, et.al., 2020). Along with:

- Affective signals, characterized as lowered satisfaction or attitude towards the job.
- Cognitive signals, linked to expressing cynicism about one's work role, or showing signs of distrust towards management, and colleagues.
- Behavioral signals, defined by reduced effectiveness, reduced work performance and one's productivity, high turnover within the organization, absenteeism, increased sick leave, accidents or showing signs of over dependence on supervisors.
- Motivational signs, related to loss of work motivation, resistance to attend work, and general low morale (Korunka, et.al., 2020).

Although there can be a variety of symptoms of burnout manifesting within the individual it also appears to be a process that goes through different escalating stages. Researchers seem to not agree about the specific order of these stages or symptoms within them (Korunka, et.al., 2020; Bursich, 2006). The basic aspects of the burnout process may be "presumed" in the following stages (Korunka, et.al., 2020; Bursich, 2006).

Four Stages of Burnout in Symptoms Manifestation

Stage one: Employees usually experience high levels of workload, job stress and job expectation. Thus job demands exceed job resources, and the job doesn't fulfil one's expectation.

Stage two: Employees usually feel physical and emotional exhaustion, which becomes chronic exhaustion. At this stage employees continuously invest higher and higher levels of energy to get the tasks done. This manifests on bodily functions causing sleep disturbances, susceptibility to headaches, or other pains.

Stage three: One may experience depersonalization, cynicism, and indifference. This may show in a form of apathy, depression, boredom, negative attitude towards the job, colleagues or other people whom the employee comes in contact with. Eventually this leads to withdrawal from work, and reduced work effort.

Stage four: An employee goes through despair, sense of helplessness, and aversion, experienced to oneself, other people or things, and accompanied with feelings of guilt and insufficiency (Korunka, et.al., 2020).

Gaborova

The following sections present recommendations for employers, managers/team, leaders/supervisors, and individuals. The guides can be used to explore culture change and activities that enable well-being for individuals, and ultimately help to reduce stressors that may lead to burnout.

The three sections are:

1. Employer - GREEN
2. Team Leader - BLUE
3. Individual - RED

I

Has your organization experienced employee burnout?

Burnout is classified as an occupational phenomenon. It is not a medical condition (11th Revision of the International Classification of Diseases, ICD-11). The World Health Organization (WHO, 2019) characterized burn-out syndrome as "a result from chronic workplace stress that has not been successfully managed". It is characterized by three dimensions:

- Emotional exhaustion: feelings of energy depletion;
- Depersonalization: increased mental distance from one's job, or feelings of negativism or cynicism related to one's job;
- Lack of accomplishment: reduced professional efficacy.

Understanding burnout is a first fundamental step to change.

2

Has employee dissatisfaction, which may lead to

burnout, become an issue

within your work environment?

It may be daunting to discuss, but it's a fact that statistically burnout is on the rise!

➢ Begin by measuring burnout. Use for example Maslach's burnout inventory: https://www.mindgarden.com/maslach-burnout-inventory-mbi/172-mbi-remote-online-survey-license.html

➢ Managers/supervisors play a significant role in your employees' well-being; train them to be empathic helpful mentors, and a source for growth and career development.

Management commitment is a catalyst for fostering positive transformation.

3

Do your employees have all the resources needed to accomplish their work?

If you are not sure, meet with work teams to determine their needs, and increase support through various methods:

➢ Share your strategic vision with the company.
➢ Give employees more autonomy (encourage independence, creativity, self-interests).
➢ Create a culture of positive, supportive, professional relationships among the colleagues (via team building get-togethers, or outside of work fun /leisure/well-being activities).
➢ Provide opportunities for growth and excellence (workshops, professional development, training that is both challenging and meaningful).
➢ Offer regular feedback, provide a comfortable space for employees to ask questions or to ask for help, Meetings shall be frequent, relevant, and motivating.

Investing in your employees provides motivation, energy and fuel to do their work.

4

Are you aware of specific job demands that require sustained effort and energy?

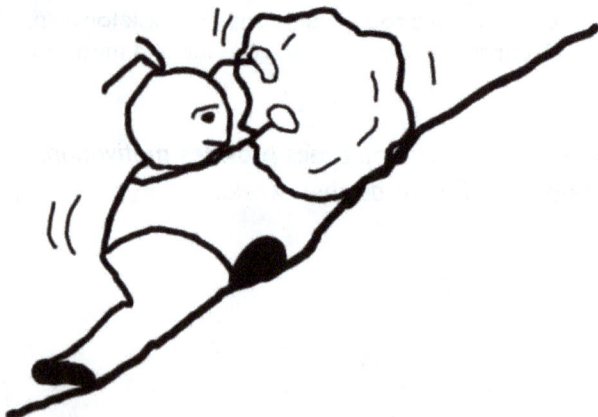

Engage your employees in open discussions to minimize some of the job demands, such as:

- role ambiguity related to unclear expectations of someone's work objectives and duties; and
- role conflicts related to conflicting requests from more than one person;
- unfair/unequal treatment of employees (refer to green Guide 5).

Corrective measures taken will increase employee satisfaction as well as work productivity.

5

Do your employees FEEL that they are being fairly treated?

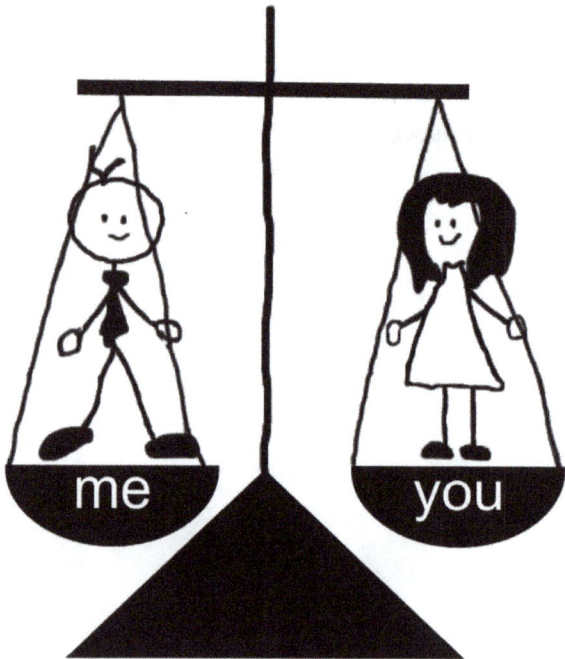

Justice in a workplace includes these four dimensions:

- distributive justice related to fair share (equity, equality, need),
- procedural justice related to implementing fair treatment and generating unbiased decisions,
- informational justice related to timeliness, specificity, and truthfulness, and
- interpersonal justice related to the treatment received, providing explanations for decisions, showing sensitivity, dignity, courtesy and respect.

A supportive workplace offers: a support person during difficult conversations, or managerial meetings, fair and available complaint-handling procedures, privacy and confidentiality, empathy training for managers, and how to avoid blame/criticism.

Work with employees to enable a culture based on JUST decision-making.

6

Is there ongoing or increasing conflict between employees and /or with supervisors?

Could this be due to an unmanageable workload, low resources, micro-management, exhaustion?

If the answer is "possibly"….

➢ Invest in workshops focused on training democratic leaders;
➢ Promote open communication amongst all employees and leaders;
➢ Promote a culture that values disagreements and differing opinions, and seeks respectful suggestions on improvements;
➢ Hire an on-site trained professional, a person who can explore solutions and support employees when facing challenging issues;
➢ Promote physical and mental well-being by having campaigns/workshops; and
➢ Express gratitude to your employees with a recognition reward appropriate to the event and of their choice: bonus, time off, training, gift voucher, thank you guides.

Compounding positive change at every level will make a difference.

7

Does your company offer flexible work

arrangements for employees?

Flexible work arrangements for employees enable a better balance of their work and personal lives, and include:

- working from home,
- on-site versus on-line options, and
- alternating schedules with flexible hours of employment give employees more control over their schedules.

Flexible work arrangements increase job satisfaction and motivation while lowering employees' stress levels.

Happy employees = Happy boss ☺

8

Are employees overwhelmed by work overload,

or adversely, unchallenged by

low work demands?

Workload refers to the level of effort that is required over time. Workload may include:

- the volume of work that needs to be done on a shift: e.g. number of boxes to unpack, number of reports to analyze;
- the difficulty of the work: e.g. size and weight per box, complexity of data reporting;
- the intensity of the work: meeting deadlines;
- the pace of the work: e.g. scheduled breaks, continuous work; and
- the number of hours worked in a day (8) or a week (40, 50).

Both work overload and underload may be stressful and increase negative emotions.

Seek input from your employees to determine an efficient process and a good balance to accomplish work requirements.

9

Are employee roles and responsibilities clearly defined within your organization or working environment?

Effective work descriptions enable employee satisfaction which in turn lowers staff turnover. Some recommendations include:

➢ Guide and coordinate employees' work activities;
➢ Set task-oriented objectives in work groups (refer to blue guide no. 13);
➢ Discuss work requirements, including duties and responsibilities with employees;
➢ Encourage alternate efficient ways of working;
➢ Reward the innovative/effective/productive nature of employees;
➢ Evaluate performance by providing a transparent benchmark for comparison;
➢ Track employees' progress on a regular basis (weekly, monthly, or yearly); and
➢ Provide positive, constructive feedback (meetings, workshops).

Having specific and clearly defined roles, and offering a positive work environment makes employees feel more accomplished, less burned out and wanting to stay.

10

Do your employees have autonomy and control over their own work?

Job autonomy and control is related to flexibility and control over how the work is accomplished. This can be achieved through various methods:

➢ Place performance metrics and expectations within employees' control;

➢ Track their achievements (refer to green guide no. 9);

➢ Have regular one-on-one conversations to discuss how your employees are doing;

➢ Reward or offer incentives for improvements made or milestones attained;

➢ Provide peaceful working environments with few distractions;

➢ Work requirements permitting, allow employees to choose where and when they will work (on site, at home, office location close to home, etc.);

➢ Promote calmness and positive emotions through natural lighting and by adding plants; and

➢ Provide spaces where employees can connect.

The more employees feel autonomous and in control, the more they feel a sense of freedom which in turn increases work satisfaction and decreases possibility of burnout.

II

Do you or your team members feel any pressure or face challenges in completing work assignments due to a lack of resources?

If yes, then meet with the team to determine issues and to rethink the methodology:

➢ Evaluate systems or processes, keeping those that work well and are still beneficial.
➢ Change systems or processes that are inefficient.
➢ Should non-beneficial systems be automated, better documented or replaced?
➢ Determine with your team members/colleagues if there are unrealistic timelines, resources, budgets, and/or workload.
➢ Work requirements permitting, determine additional time for each deadline to reduce the pressure.

Still struggling? Hire an organizational coach or psychologist to assess the work environment and to provide suggestions for more effective/supportive cooperation.

12

Do you or your team members

easily ask for help?

Sometimes life/work feels too overwhelming. Create an environment where it's easy to ask for help, more time or extra resources. Open communication may show where there are difficulties that could be resolved by offering extra mentoring, support, or resources.

An example of 'how' to ask for help is to express your feeling, describe the situation and express what you need to 'fix' the problem, a formula (I feel, about, need) as inspired by "The complaint formula" (from the Gottman Institute):

"Lately I have been feeling….(e.g. overwhelmed, exhausted, frustrated), about (name the situation, e.g. the work requirements, software problems, lack of training,…), and I was hoping that (express the need, e.g. we could examine the process, assess the difficulties…)".

If a colleague asks for help, determine how you can help them or what advice can you give to resolve the issue. Remember that it takes a lot of courage to ask for help. This courage needs to be acknowledged with a positive outcome or a solution to the problems.

13

Do you or your team members know precisely
the tasks expected of each of you at work?

Stress or burnout may be more prevalent if there is ambiguity or lack of clear expectations related to the tasks.

➢ Have open communication with your team leader/supervisor/colleagues about specifics, and expectations related to roles and responsibilities.
➢ Ask questions, specify deadlines and priorities, provide examples, offer mentoring, set up mini-goals, recheck on clarity (Refer to green guide no. 9).

Clear expectations increase efficiency and constructive effort.

14

When basic needs are met, individuals can
achieve a higher level of self-actualization.
Do you or your team members
feel that your needs are met?

Humans feel more depleted of energy when they sacrifice their own needs and want to try to satisfy others.

- A loss of vitality can leave someone feeling hurt, exhausted, physically uncomfortable, resentful or angry.
- Organize a 'body language' workshop for your team, learn to read body sensations, identify physical, emotional, and mental boundaries, and determine a signal if these get crossed.

Maslow's Hierarchy of Needs (1943, 1954) categorizes the five basic levels of the hierarchy of needs of individuals as basic needs that include physiological (e.g. food, sleep), and safety (e.g. shelter, health/financial security); psychological needs - love/belonging (e.g. social connection, intimacy), esteem (e.g. recognition, achievement, status); and self-fulfillment needs - self-actualization (e.g. morality, fulfillment). Behaviors are usually motivated by multiple needs simultaneously. Lower levels of "basic/survival" needs are met before the higher "creative or intellectually oriented" needs can be fulfilled.

Team members will be stronger and more productive when their needs are met.

15

Does imperfection frustrate you

or your colleagues?

Being a perfectionist increases anxiety, releases the inner critical voice, makes people feel "not good enough" and could lead to burnout. When possible encourage the team to adopt a "good enough approach":

➢ Be more effective with a "good enough" approach.
➢ Apply the Pareto Principle (known as the 80/20 rule) for guidance. With this principle individuals and organizations can improve efficiency, productivity, and effectiveness by focusing on the most critical high-impact areas, solving the most critical problems or allocating the most substantial resources that drive the majority of results.
➢ Offer a workshop to increase awareness of perfectionist tendencies, to identify the progress or the positives related to anyone's work.
➢ Identify the smaller goals achieved and what was learnt through the process.
➢ Redirect the focus on the meaning/purpose or the process of work or learning rather than perfection.
➢ Train yourself and others to do jobs immediately, as a rough draft and then work your way towards improvements rather than procrastinating because of wanting perfection.

"The pursuit of perfection often impedes improvement"

— George Will 1941 -

16

Have you or your colleagues been challenged, transformed or learned anything new?

Learning new activities or mentally demanding skills improves:

- Cognitive functioning, slows down aging, improves memory and decreases boredom.
- Personal growth/learning boosts confidence, self-esteem, general well-being, and gives a sense of happiness and satisfaction.
- Offer internal programs that encourage colleagues to exchange jobs within departments, or arrange for employees to shadow other employees to learn new skills. Have employees mentor others to teach and learn new skills.

If you or your colleagues could learn something new...what would it be? Ask for everyone's input and mutually choose what would benefit the group.

17

Have you or your colleagues been working
overtime, or working from home
after work hours?

Does the work environment respect official work schedules or does it have a culture that expects employees to work during their off time? Are the extra hours worked compensated by overtime pay or time off in lieu of pay?

- Are you expected to answer the phone or finalize reports during your free time, off days, sick leave or on vacation?
- Are you working past your scheduled time because most of your colleagues do it too?

Working overtime shall not become a norm. Overwork of 50-55 hours/per week and above was found to decline: cognitive abilities, productivity, health, creativity (Westover, 2023).

Extra working hours shall be meticulously planned and requested only with mutual agreement when the task genuinely requires overtime. Compensation for these additional hours needs to be fair, either through financial bonuses or equivalent time off. Otherwise, the work requirements, processes, or number of employees to complete the work shall be reevaluated.

18

Are you or your colleagues practicing activities that help reduce stress levels?

You may do this on your own, or with your colleagues. Do the stress reducers below sound familiar? It is advantageous for your team to learn from a workshop or training session about self-care, chronic stress awareness, burnout, and stress reduction techniques, such as:

- breathing exercises,
- guided meditation,
- hypnosis,
- muscle-tension relaxation techniques,
- mindfulness,
- using aromatherapy diffusors in the office space,
- massage chairs, or gift vouchers for massage, self-care products, and
- exercise, stretches or walks during working hours.

Engage with your co-workers by sharing your favourite techniques, and feel free to add your own suggestions to the list.

19

Have you or your colleagues sent a positive

message/appreciation note

to another team member today?

A simple thank you, or any words of appreciation, could be sent to a different colleague each day.

Be creative with your positive message; show appreciation for something:

- inspiring about that person,
- that person taught you,
- this person did to help you, and/or
- this person did to make your day more pleasant.

Kind words of appreciation increase a sense of happiness, positivity, and strengthen social connections within your team. Encourage the team to develop a culture of appreciation.

"It is not joy that makes us grateful; it is gratitude that makes us joyful."

—David Steinall-Rast 1926 -

20

Have you or your colleagues discussed and practiced saying 'no' when work demands are overwhelming or when you cannot meet the deadline?

Saying 'yes' to increased work expectations, when you do not mean it or against your inclination, results in crossing one's own personal boundaries. The outcome is feeling exhausted, stressed or even burnt out. Learn to say 'no':

➢ Create a team norm that allows a pause to reflect before saying 'yes' immediately;

➢ Let each team member check whether the task is doable or too overwhelming, and at the cost of sacrificing one's own needs or well-being;

➢ Teach the team to say: "I will check my schedule, and will get back to you soon" to reduce the pressure and keep everyone aware of their own needs; and

➢ Explore solutions/compromises together and reflect on other ways for completing the work.

Encouraging team members to see situations through their colleagues' eyes can enhance overall understanding.

" *Just because you don't understand it doesn't mean it isn't so.*"

— *Lemony Snicket 1970 -*

21

Does the work environment allow for team
members to stand up for themselves
and their beliefs?

Practicing assertiveness is an important ingredient for protecting one's personal boundaries:

➢ Offer your team members training or one-on-one sessions with an organizational coach;
➢ Have workshops on awareness of personal boundaries, the optimal workload, increased effectiveness while practicing regular self-care, etc.;
➢ Build confidence by first practicing assertiveness in less challenging situations (e.g. on a colleague with whom you feel the most comfortable); work your way up towards the greater challenges, and
➢ Play your argument over in your mind to determine various responses.

Assertiveness training will increase open communication amongst team members, help to keep the workload in check, and allow everyone to express their own opinions, beliefs and thoughts in a respectful manner.

Can you imagine situations where assertiveness would reduce work stress?

22

Do you and your team members promote
a culture that values health and exercise?

Any form of aerobic exercise, at least 3-4 times per week for a minimum of 30 minutes per session, will boost serotonin levels in your body. Aerobic exercise:

- reduces stress,
- improves mood due to increased serotonin production,
- increases cognitive abilities,
- strengthens immune system, and
- increases overall physical and mental health.

If you are not used to exercising or have started feeling symptoms of burnout:

➤ take small steps starting with little effort, then slowly and gradually increase the exercise;
➤ discuss the type, frequency and intensity with a physiotherapist; and
➤ ask your leaders for gym space at work, purchase a gym membership, or walk at lunch break.

Exercise is a natural serotonin booster that beats any prescription. ☺

23

Do you or your team members feel trapped
or out of control due to workload?

Human beings like to have their lives under control. There are two ways of coping: approaching or avoiding.

➢ Approaching is the more effective coping mechanism. Approaching the work and breaking the tasks into smaller achievable sub-tasks will increase the sense of having more control. Ask "can anything influence or control this situation", e.g. extra time to meet deadline, more resources, consultation with an expert? If yes, do it.
➢ Frustrating as it appears, accepting the situation and moving your focus onto other tasks that can still be influenced, is more productive. Accept the challenge.
➢ Review tasks regularly following the SMART model (https://corporatefinanceinstitute.com/resources/management/smart-goal/)

Choosing avoidance brings unexpected consequences that could make matters worse, e.g. unfinished project/task, losing control over your decisions, increase production costs, etc.

24

Do you and your members conduct activities aligned with your personal ethics, morals and values?

Doing activities that are true to one's own values feels like a navigator is directing a smoother ride to the destination. In fact ...

- Aligned values motivate, lead to a sense of accomplishment, and decrease stress and burnout (see Resources; e.g. doing the tasks with a purpose/mission that resonates strongly with own personal beliefs);
- Actions that are nonaligned with personal core values may increase internal pressures, lack of integrity and confusion, thus contributing to burnout.

"Values are like fingertips. Nobody's are the same, but you leave them all over everything you do".

—— *Elvis Presley 1935-1977*

25

Do you or your team members express negative

attitudes towards others,

especially when facing change?

Some examples of negative attitudes and their antidotes include:

- Self-defeating talk, apply antidote: use encouraging talk by offering positive reinforcement, praise, and constructive feedback to inspire confidence, perseverance, and growth.
- Critical assumptions, apply antidote: stick to the facts, evaluate both the positive and negative sides objectively. What can you learn from this process?
- Undermining comparison with others, apply antidote: check your own progress from the point or time you started.
- Rumination about the past, apply antidote: ask "*can I do anything about it?*" If yes, go and do what needs to be done. If not, practice acceptance. Preserve your energy for things that you can still change.
- Blaming yourself repeatedly, apply antidote: mistakes happen. What can I learn from this mistake?
- Fear of failure, apply antidote: each set back increases one's own psychological immunity and resilience. Each trial teaches something new, and increases your efficacy for the future. What helped you to survive your challenging moments? Are these evidence of your own resilience and growth?

26

Are you experiencing prolonged unrestful
or insufficient sleep?

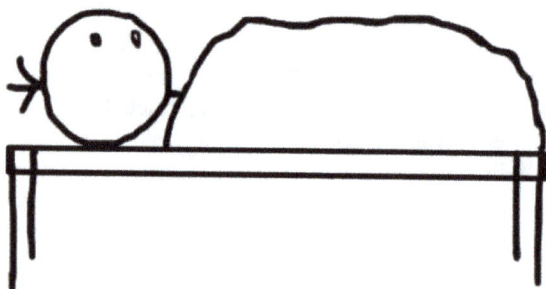

"I want to sleep but my brain won't stop talking to itself" (Anonymous). Sounds familiar?

At night:

➢ Prepare your room for sleep (no light, cool temperature),
➢ Do not eat heavy food before bed,
➢ Use lavender oils, shower gels, or bath salts before sleep,
➢ Write down things that worry you or you do not want to forget, and
➢ Do a breathing, or meditation exercise.
➢ If insomnia persists consult with a sleep CBT specialist.

Morning routine:

➢ Get up 15 minutes before your usual time, even if you went to bed late,
➢ Start your day with a short relaxation technique (see blue guide no. 18),
➢ Drink herbal tea (chamomile, valerian or lavender) during the day, and
➢ Do at least 30 minutes of aerobic physical exercise 3-4 times per week.

Breathe in the peace, breathe out the worries...

27

Are you 'flowing' through life
or continuously depleting yourself?

The term "Flow" was introduced by Dr Mihaly Cszikzentmihalyi in the 1970's, describing it as an *optimal state of being*, being open, consciously attentive to the stream of life when interacting with the environment. The opposite of a flow is depleting oneself. Which attitude best describes you? Sometimes? All of the time?

Two attitudes to work (based on Sonja van Zweden's work)

	FLOW	DEPLETING YOURSELF
Orientation	Quality, the work is going well	Quantity and result are foremost, the work needs to be finished
Result	Process	Product
Compass	Internal Personal tempo Personal rhythm Personal organisation Variety	External Pressure Commands/control Adapting/forcing oneself Continuing for too long
Energy	Providing	Demanding
Concentration	Fully	Disturbed
Motivation	Willingness, enjoying, appreciating. It comes from yourself	Feeling forced or compelled, doing because others want you to; recognition from others
Experience	Creative	Monotonous
Recovery	Completely	Partly
Limits	Own happiness and well-being	It needs to be finished; continuing until you drop

28

Are you often too busy to take a break?

Our brains operate on two modes: a focused mode is mostly used for learning, working, writing, etc. and a diffused mode is related to a relaxed or dreamy state.

Guess when breakthroughs appear out of nowhere? Absolutely! They are often a product of a diffused brain mode. In fact, many people get their best ideas when they are sleeping!

Taking a break:

- Gives you valuable insights and improves mood;
- Recharges you to return to a productivity zone, to refocus; and
- Encourages you to stay mindful of objectives and to think globally.

If possible, try to work 90 minutes followed by a 20-minute break, which is our basic rate activity cycle. If this is not possible use the Pomodoro technique. Apply a Pomodoro cycle: work 25 minutes and break for five minutes. Choose the best cycle of productivity that works for you. Do you notice a difference?

Refer to Appendix A: Human Factors Lab research study aimed to address meeting fatigue in remote and hybrid work.

29

Do you sometimes/often feel physically
or emotionally exhausted?

Remove or at least minimize any stressors (see blue guide no. 18):

➤ Clear your schedule;
➤ Make a date with yourself in your calendar each day if you are too busy to take a break;
➤ Plan or extend a vacation;
➤ Do not eat at your desk;
➤ Spend time outside; and
➤ Let others spoil you.

Moments of relaxation will help reverse feelings of exhaustion.

30

Have you been suffering from more pains
(head/neck/back), fatigue, or illnesses
(colds, inflammation, high blood pressure,
heart palpitations) lately?

Chronic stress and burnout may increase muscle tension, thus increasing body pain.

➢ Talk to your general practitioner or naturopath (stress may cause a shortage of vitamins and minerals e.g. magnesium, calcium, vitamin D & C).
➢ Schedule an appointment with a physiotherapist to plan an exercise regime and gain support.
➢ Meet with a therapist or a coach with whom you can talk about your stresses in depth.
➢ Apply ice and have warm baths to ease muscle pains (with recommendation of a physiotherapist).
➢ Keep a journal of your stressors and their solutions that work for you,
➢ Practice relaxation (see blue guide no. 18).

"Just when you feel you have no time to relax, know that this is the moment you most need to make time to relax"

— Matt Haig 1975 -

31

Have you stopped laughing or enjoying most of your usual activities? Do you prefer being alone, and avoid seeing family or friends?

A good laugh exercises the muscles, boosts immunity, increases blood flow, decreases blood pressure, helps to sleep better and decreases stress hormones.

- ➤ Spend time with those who make you laugh;
- ➤ Watch a funny movie or stand-up comedy, read a funny book, etc.;
- ➤ Take some time to rest (see blue guide no. 18);
- ➤ Experiment with 'Laughter yoga: laughing away the stress' (Youtube); and
- ➤ Signal to colleagues that you need a laugh.

"Through humor, you can soften some of the worst blows that life delivers. And once you find laughter, no matter how painful your situation might be, you can survive."

– Bill Cosby 1937 -

32

Are you more forgetful or easily distracted lately?

How to combat forgetfulness (appointments, tasks)?

➤ Speak to your doctor to rule out any physical symptoms;
➤ Rest, practice relaxation (see blue guide no. 18);
➤ Exercise regularly; plan your exercise -- type, frequency and intensity, with a physiotherapist if suffering from burnout;
➤ Sleep more;
➤ Carry a notebook and write things down;
➤ Link information with a relevant image that you can remember easily; and
➤ Organize 'to do' lists based on priorities.

"The only thing faster than the speed of thought is the speed of forgetfulness. Good thing we have other people to help us remember".

— *Vera Nazarian 1966 -*

33

Is your focus or concentration less intense than it used to be?

Practice some of the following suggestions for at least 1-2 months:

➢ Speak to your doctor to rule out any physical symptoms;
➢ Eliminate distractions;
➢ Avoid multitasking and focus on one task at a time;
➢ Practice mindfulness (see red guide no. 34);
➢ Take regular short breaks;
➢ Divide big tasks into smaller steps;
➢ Exercise (see blue guide no. 22); and
➢ Practice short term and long-term memory daily (e.g. play problem-solving games, brain stimulating videos, memory guides, puzzles etc.).

Have you noticed improvements? Chart your progress in a notebook/calendar, celebrate your success.

34

Have you accomplished any tasks consciously

or mindfully today?

By practicing mindfulness you increase your immunity, decrease anxiety, stress levels, and burnout, and uplift your mood.

Practicing mindfulness involves:

- Letting go of any judgements. Life isn't only black and white ... right or wrong;
- Sitting patiently and observing within yourself and out around you;
- Getting in touch with 'right here', 'right now' by truly seeing, feeling, hearing, smelling, tasting, and experiencing; and
- If you cannot change something, what do you need to do for you to accept the situation?

"Acceptance is challenging but it is the opposite of resistance. Giving in completely, both physically and mentally, allowing everything to flow over us—our thoughts, feelings, and sensations. Time assists with healing."

— Dr. Claire Weekes 1903-1990

35

Have you noticed your thoughts today?

Our brain is very sensitive to negative messages, thoughts, and stimuli. It is an in-built protective mechanism which may lead us to develop certain irrational thoughts or beliefs.

Did you know that thoughts influence feelings and vice versa? While practicing journaling, notice:

- Whether your thoughts/beliefs are biased opinions or facts;
- Whether there is evidence that your thoughts/beliefs either support or do not validate your thinking;
- Whether your thoughts/beliefs are helpful in reaching your goals; and
- Whether your thoughts/beliefs create unnecessary conflict or stress inside you.

When catastrophic biased thoughts and beliefs lead to unnecessary stress and conflict, ask yourself, "Is there also a possibility of a best-case scenario?" If so, strive to identify it and evaluate its potential to alleviate distress.

More information and wellness tools are available from Katarina Gaborova:
https://www.psychologistinthehague.com

36

What have you done to improve your physical health and wellbeing today?

Develop healthy habits to feel better:

➤ Say no to processed foods, eat a healthy diet (e.g. the Mediterranean diet);

➤ Drink enough liquids (around 2 liters of water per day);

➤ Have a regular intake of nutrients and vitamins; (discuss with health care professional)

➤ Cut out any alcohol or substance use;

➤ Create a routine of regular sleep time, even for the weekends. Aim for 7-9 hours of sleep if possible. Consider your chronotype (morning vs evening)(see red guide no. 26);

➤ Exercise regularly, minimum 30 minutes, 3-4 times per week;

➤ Schedule a preventive checkup by your general practitioner;

➤ Minimize your stress (see blue guide no. 18); and

➤ Prioritize sleep quality to waken refreshed and alert.

➤ Participate in activities that help your body to rest physically (have a bubble bath, short nap, massage, sauna etc.)

➤ If needed give rest to your senses and overstimulation (detach from social media, news, TV series, music or noises). Our sensory systems also need rest. If too overstimulated they may affect concentration, contribute to anxiety, irritability, restlessness, muscle tensions, increase challenges with sleep, affect digestion, etc.

37

What have you done to improve
your mental health today?

How are you feeling? Check in with yourself on a regular basis.

Lately, have you felt: happiness, sadness, stress, admiration, appreciation, amusement, anger, anxiety, awkwardness, boredom, calmness, confusion, craving, disgust, pain, excitement, fear, horror, interest, joy, nostalgia, relief, romance, satisfaction, surprise…any other emotion? Try to remember the event and the feeling.

➢ Adopt a healthy diet (learn how the gut-brain axis affects our mood and overall health).
➢ Keep a healthy sleep hygiene.
➢ Talk/vent about your worries/concerns to reduce your stress.
➢ Write 3 positive experiences of your day each evening.
➢ Describe one positive experience for 2 minutes (what you felt, saw, smelled, tasted – recall will help savor your experience once again). Gratitude activities and practices can positively stimulate the amygdala (a region of the brain associated with emotions).
➢ Participate in activities to rest emotionally (reflect on your thoughts, feelings, impressions, spirituality, creativity). If you need help, have a chat with an understanding friend/family member/therapist/coach-someone who can listen and if needed guide you.
➢ Take a social rest, a quiet moment away from others after busy social encounters.

38

Do you have a strong critical inner voice,

or do you blame yourself most of the time?

Practice talking to yourself like you would to your best friend. What advice would you give?

➤ Ask yourself why you feel as you do and how to shift criticism to encouragement.
➤ Is it time for adjustments? Be kind to yourself. Look up compassion exercises such as the Loving-Kindness Meditation/Metta, where individuals repeat phrases of well-wishes and kindness towards themselves and others.
➤ Nurture a consistent respectful inner voice.

39

What activities recharge your batteries
and energize you?

Try some of the activities listed to see if your energy level increases. Note what energizes you the most:

➢ Practice relaxation techniques (breathing exercises, muscle-tension relaxations, mindfulness, hypnosis, meditations);
➢ Spend time with friends or family, volunteer;
➢ Pursue hobbies, sports, fun events, leisure/recreation;
➢ Walk in the wind;
➢ Spend time in nature e.g. at the beach, walk in a forest, visit a park;
➢ Travel to new destinations;
➢ Visit museums, explore villages; and
➢ Acquire knowledge/information/wisdom/learning.

"The energy of the mind is the essence of life."

— Aristotle, The Works of Aristotle (4th century BC)

Source: www.blinkist.com/

40

What causes you the most stress?

Analyze your stress by keeping a record or journal of the date, time, situation, feelings, and their intensity. Stressors could include:

- work, career, study,
- changes in profession,
- colleagues, friends,
- family member, family event,
- romantic relationship,
- hobbies, fun, leisure/recreation,
- surroundings / environment,
- new experiences,
- travels,
- finances,
- personal growth / health,
- health of others,
- living condition,
- anything else?

Stress can be understood by the acronym 'NUTS': N - novelty, U - unpredictability, T - threat , and S - sense of control is low.
(https://heartmindonline.org/resources/nuts-understanding-stress)

Do you recognize any patterns or a relationship between the acronym and your stressors?

41

Are you seeing friends or family members frequently?

Social connections contribute to a sense of happiness, calmness and overall well-being that even prolongs life - a phenomenon known as the "Roseto Effect" which is "widely cited as evidence for the positive effects of social cohesion and social support on longevity." (Brenda Egolif, Judith Lasker, Stewart Wolf, and Louise Potvin. *The Roseto Effect: A 50-Year Comparison of Mortality Rates* (1992).)

Social connections include activities such as:

- family events,
- group picnics,
- volunteering in the community, soup kitchens,
- visiting with seniors,
- mentoring / training youth,
- get-togethers with friends,
- book / reading clubs, and
- outdoor walking / biking / sports clubs.

Reach out to those who make you feel safe, and whom you can count on.

42

Do you feel more depleted of energy, angry
or stressed around certain people?

When facing a stressful situation, shield yourself from negativity by visualizing something you love or are looking forward to.

➢ Take a mental/physical distance from the source of stress by looking at nature, an object in the room (e.g. a plant, painting on the wall, etc.) or see yourself as a detached observer.
➢ Talk or vent to a person with whom you feel comfortable.
➢ Slow down your breathing (< 12 breaths /minute).
➢ Set clear boundaries.
➢ Imagine the conversation and anticipate a positive outcome.
➢ Plan something fun for yourself each day after work so that you can anticipate feeling joyful.

Protecting yourself mentally will increase your self-assurance.

43

Are you repeatedly feeling that 'time is too slow' as you work to the end of your shift, or fear that 'time really flies' as the pressure builds to finish your work on schedule?

Clock-watching may increase stress levels; whether you feel time dragging on or flying, pressure builds each time you are aware of time passing. This may actually leave less time to do the actual work. Change your behavior by first ignoring the clock, and

➢ Give structure to your work;
➢ Make a plan/'to do' list and prioritize only important matters;
➢ Critically evaluate whether the task is still necessary or relevant;
➢ Throughout the day -- work, rest, work, rest, work, rest;
➢ Remove distractions (e.g. phone, non-work related emails);
➢ Set specific times to respond to emails (improves efficiency); and
➢ Leave work on time (set an alarm 30 minutes prior to your departure).

Internal Alarm Clock: A One-Week Challenge

Human bodies have an internal alarm clock that regulates basic physiological needs like eating, drinking, resting, and sleeping. Unlike other living creatures, humans often ignore these essential needs, whether by staying up until 5 a.m. to finish a TV series, eating out of social obligation rather than hunger, or pushing through exhaustion despite clear signs that rest is needed. This self-neglect adds unnecessary stress to our lives.

To reconnect with your body's natural signals, try a one-week experiment where you actively listen to and follow your body's cues. Treat yourself as you would a newborn, carefully observing and responding to your needs.

At the end of the week, reflect:

- Did you notice a significant improvement in your overall well-being?
- Do you feel energized?
- Have your eating and sleeping habits provided you with more strength and motivation?

Gaborova

I hope that this journey through "Tools to Prevent Burnout, The Invigorate Model" provides new insights, contributes to rebuilding your resilience, and enables a new sense of self-compassion.

In addition to the ideas from this book, you might consider exploring self-regulatory biofeedback training. This technique involves using electronic monitoring to convey information about physiological processes, such as cardiac functioning, and is used to learn how to control these processes to manage stress and reduce burnout symptoms (May et al., 2018).

You could also explore various types of hydrotherapy, such as warm baths, geothermal mineral waters, or alternating hot and cold water treatments, to alleviate stress and fatigue. A study investigating the effects of high-salinity geothermal mineral water on stress and fatigue found that balneotherapy significantly reduced stress-related symptoms, pain, and fatigue while improving mood, motivation, and cognitive function (Rapoliene et al., 2016).

Please remember that in the depths of any emotional and physical exhaustion also lies an opportunity for new growth, rejuvenation of the body, and self-discovery. Honor your personal boundaries, nurture your well-being, and continuously cultivate a sense of balance of your mind, body, and spirit.

May this book serve as a guiding light, filled with vitality, joy, hope, and your body's strength to rise, heal, and thrive.

— Katarina

Appendix A:
Human Factors Lab

Research study aimed to address fatigue in remote and hybrid work.

The image below shows Microsoft's recent study conducted by the Human Factors Lab. Researchers aimed to address meeting fatigue in the context of remote and hybrid work. Using electroencephalogram (EEG) equipment on 14 participants who engaged in video meetings, alternating between sessions of back-to-back half-hour meetings and sessions with 10-minute meditation breaks between meetings. The study aimed to compare cognitive responses and well-being outcomes between the two meeting formats while maintaining consistency in downtime activities for clean data analysis.

The research identified three main findings:

1) Breaks between meetings facilitate a brain "reset," preventing the accumulation of stress across consecutive meetings. Therefore, taking short breaks is essential to combat meeting fatigue.

2) Back-to-back meetings reduce focus and engagement. Meditation breaks result in positive brainwave patterns linked to higher engagement, while lack of breaks leads to negative patterns, indicating decreased engagement. Therefore, breaks not only benefit well-being but also enhance performance.

3) Transitioning between meetings can induce high stress, especially for those without breaks. The period between calls can cause spikes in beta wave activity, reflecting heightened stress levels as individuals prepare to switch tasks. However, taking meditation breaks mitigates this stress response, resulting in smoother transitions and reduced beta activity between meetings.

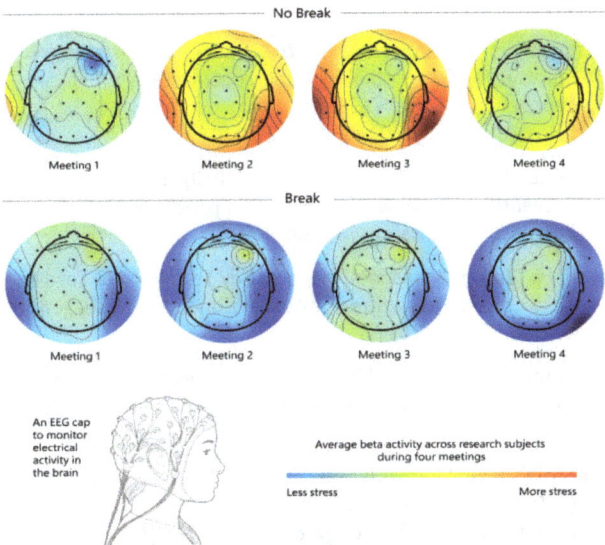

No Break

Meeting 1   Meeting 2   Meeting 3   Meeting 4

Break

Meeting 1   Meeting 2   Meeting 3   Meeting 4

An EEG cap to monitor electrical activity in the brain

Average beta activity across research subjects during four meetings

Less stress   More stress

Note: Beta waves (a type of electrical activity) in the brain are higher-frequency brain waves that are characteristic of active, alert, and engaged mental states. They are most prominent when the brain is actively processing information, such as during problem-solving, decision-making, or focused attention. Beta waves are generally associated with heightened cognitive activity and can indicate states of stress or anxiety when excessively present.

Resources

Alarcon, G., Eschleman, K., & Bowling, N.A. (2009). Relationships between personality variables and burnout: A meta-analysis. *An international Journal of Work, Health, & Organisations, 23 (3)*, 243-263.

Angelini, G. (2023). Big five model personality traits and job burnout: A systematic literature review. *BMC Psychology, 11(49).* https://doi.org/10.1186/s40359-023-00745-y

Arnsten, A. F. T., & Shanafelt, T. (2021). Physician distress and burnout: The neurobiological perspective. Mayo Clinic Proceedings, 96(3), 763-769. https://doi.org/10.1016/j.mayocp.2020.12.022

Awa, W.L., Plaumann, M., &Walter, U. (2010). Burnout prevention: a review of intervention programs. *Patient Educational Counselling 78*, 184–190.

Cloud, H. (2002). *Boundaries: When to Say Yes, When to Say No, To Take Control of Your Life.* Publisher. Zondervan; Enlarged edition (2 Nov. 2017).

Csikszentmihalyi, Mihaly (1975). Beyond Boredom and Anxiety: Experiencing Flow in Work and Play, San Francisco: Jossey-Bass.

Demerouti, E.; Bakker, A.B.; Nachreiner, F.; &Schaufeli, W.B. (2001). The job demands- resources model of burnout. *Journal of Applied Psychology, 86*, 499–512.

Golkar, A.; Johansson, E.; Kasahara, M.; Osika, W.; Perski, A., & Savic, I. (2014). The influence of work-related chronic stress on the regulation of emotion and on functional connectivity in the brain. Downloaded in August 2022 from: https://doi.org/10.1371/journal.pone.0104550

Goodwin, J. (2023). Change Your Brain for 30 Days: Harness the Power of Neuroplasticity to Transform Your Mind and Life in Just 30 Days. Paperback edition. Amazon.

Gottman Institute – containing the guide to complaining : downloaded in 2024 from: https://www.gottman.com/blog/a-couples-guide-to-complaining/

Halbesleben, J.R. & Buckley, M.R. (2004). Burnout in organizational life. *Journal of Managment 30*, 859–879.

Hobfoll, S.E. (1989). Conservation of resources: A new attempt at conceptualizing stress. *American Psychologist, 44*, 513-524.

Karasek, R.A. (1985). *Job content questionnaire and user's guide.* Los Angeles: University of Southern California, Department of Industrial and System Engineering.

Karin, O., Raz, M., Tendler, A., Bar, A., Kohanim, Y. K., Milo, T., & Alon, U. (2020). A new model for the HPA axis explains dysregulation of stress hormones on the timescale of weeks. *Molecular Systems Biology, 16(7)*, e9510. https://doi.org/10.15252/msb.20209510

Korunka,Ch., Tement, S., Zdrehus, C., & Borza, A. (2020).Burnout: Definition, recognition and prevention approaches. Downloaded in April 2020 from: https://www.bridgestoeurope.com/wp-content/uploads/2020/03/BOIT_theoretical_abstract_2705.pdfLazarus, R., & Folkman, S. (1984). Stress, Appraisal, and Coping. New York:

Lennartsson, A.-K., Sjörs, A., Währborg, P., Ljung, T., & Jonsdottir, I. H. (2015). Burnout and Hypocortisolism – A Matter of Severity? A Study on ACTH and Cortisol Responses to Acute Psychosocial Stress. *Frontiers in Psychiatry, 6*, 8. https://doi.org/10.3389/fpsyt.2015.00008

Magnano, P., Paolillo, A., &Barrano, C. (2015). Relationships between personality and burnout: an empirical study with helping professions' workers. *International Journal of Humanities and Social Science Research, 1*, 10-19.

Maslach, C.; Leiter, M.P. (2016). Understanding the burnout experience: recent research and its implications for psychiatry. *World Psychiatry 15(2), 103-111.*

Maslow, A. H. (1943). A theory of human motivation. *Psychological Review, 50* (4), 370-96.

Maslow, A. H. (1954). Motivation and personality. New York: Harper and Row.

May, R. W., Seibert, G. S., Sanchez-Gonzalez, M. A., & Fincham, F. D. (2018). Self-regulatory biofeedback training: An intervention to reduce school burnout and improve cardiac functioning in college students. Stress: The International Journal on the Biology of Stress, 1-8. https://doi.org/10.1080/10253890.2018.1501021

McFarland, D.C., Hlubocky, F., &Riba, M. (2019). Update on addressing mental health and burnout in physicians: What is the role of psychiatry? Current Psychiatry Reports, 21, (108). https://doi.org/10.1007/s11920-019-1100-6

Microsoft. (April 20, 2021). Brain research: How the way we work is changing our brains. Microsoft WorkLab. https://www.microsoft.com/en-us/worklab/work-trend-index/brain-research

Orloff, J. (2017). The Empath's Survival Guide: Life Strategies for Sensitive People. Sounds True Inc.

Rapolienė, L., Razbadauskas, A., Sąlyga, J., & Martinkėnas, A. (2016). Stress and fatigue management using balneotherapy in a short-time randomized controlled trial. Evidence-Based Complementary and Alternative Medicine, 2016, 9631684. https://doi.org/10.1155/2016/9631684

Rostami, Z., Abedi, M. R., & Schaufeli, W. B. (2012). Does interest predict academic burnout? Interdisciplinary Journal of Contemporary Research in Business, 3(9), 877–885.

Scott, E., & Snyder, C. (2020). Traits and attitudes that increase burnout risk. Retrieved in April 2021 from: https://www.verywellmind.com/mental-burnout-personality-traits- 3144514

Sparks, D. (2021). Chronic stress can wreak havoc on your mind and body. Health & Wellness. Downloaded in January 2024 from: https://newsnetwork.mayoclinic.org/discussion/chronic-stress-can-wreak-havoc-on-your-mind-and-body/

Springer, Thau, L., Gandhi, J., & Sharma, S. (2023). Physiology, Cortisol. In StatPearls Downloaded in December 2023 from:

https://www.ncbi.nlm.nih.gov/books/NBK538239/. Last Update: August 28, 2023.

Statista Research Department. (2021, July 7). Burnout among employees in the U.S. as of July 2021, by generation. Statista. https://www.statista.com/statistics/1256283/burnout-among-us-employees-by-generation/

Van der Doef, M., & Maes, S. (1999). The job demand-control (-support) model and psychological well-being: A review of 20 years of empirical research. *Work Stress 13*, 87–114.

Westermann C., Kozak, A., Harling,M.,&Nienhaus, A. (2014). Burnout intervention studies for inpatient elderly care nursing staff: systematic literature review. *International Journal of Nursing Studies, 51, 63–71.*

Westover, J. H. (2023). Why working after hours may decrease productivity. Downloaded in May 2023 from: https://www.innovativehumancapital.com/post/why-working-after-hours-may-decrease-productivity

Willis, J. (2014, May 1). Neuroscience reveals that boredom hurts. Feature Article. Kappan. https://kappanonline.org/neuroscience-reveals-that-boredom-hurts-willis/#:~:text=Whenever%20the%20amygdalae%20are%20highly,the%20rest%20of%20the%20brain.

World Health Organization (2019). Burn-out an "occupational phenomenon": International Classification of Diseases (ICD-11). Retrieved in November 2019 from: https://www.who.int/mental_health/evidence/burn-out/en/.

Zafar, M. S., Nauman, M., Nauman, H., Nauman, S., Kabir, A., Shahid, Z., Fatima, A., & Batool, M. (2021). Impact of Stress on Human Body: A Review. *European Journal of Medical and Health Sciences (EJMED)*, v.3 no.3, 2021

Katarina Gaborova, founder of K.G. Psychological Services, based in The Hague, Netherlands, specializes in supporting individuals and couples through various mental health challenges, with a particular focus on burnout. Over the past five years, Katarina has researched burnout and has designed a series of workshops for international organizations, schools, and corporations. In addition to her private practice, she is passionate about creating inspirational books and cards (V!VA Tools for well-being, See Bee Tee products). With this book, Katarina aims to broaden awareness of burnout, enhance self-help strategies, and encourage workplaces to better support their employees. For more information on her work, education, and research, visit her websites:

https://www.katarinagaborova.com/
and
https://www.psychologistinthehague.com/